The Smile
& Other Poems

Rudy Thomas

The Smile & Other Poems
Copyright 2008 by Rudy Thomas
Old Seventy Creek Press

All rights reserved under International and Pan-American Conventions. Published in the United States, this volume is a First Edition.

ISBN 978-0-6151-9690-9

For Jamie

Acknowledgment: David Cazden, Editor, miller's pond, for publishing the poem: *Writing a novel*, 2006 Vol. 1 Issue 1, H&H Press, Middlebury Center, PA.

All the women I never loved

Book One

Sunlight on the snow

does not warm my thumbs
tho it blinds me as I walk.
Ahead of me, cardinals forage
& the wind whistles,
following the lay of the land
without leaving tracks as I do.

I remind myself to feed the birds crumbs
when I have finished my walk
& before I place words on a page
to stand tall like thistles,
protected by needles & at home on arid land.
May the words I write thrive on dew

& bloom like tall weeds come August.

My feelings are warm

as the bed
from which you rise
in the morning.

Even in winter,
warm,
tho my face is red,

chilled by morning wind,
brisk & dangerous,
from the west.

I have saved the best
of words like heirloom seeds
for spring planting. Then,

I dig them into the blank page,
running horizontal
like furrows in a garden.

Winter Night

Wind from the north
drifts snow
across the field
where the creek
with no name
flows.

As I watch
thru the A-frame
wall of glass,
the rolling hillside
turns white,
darkness falls.

I christen the stream
Muse creek.
Each time I look into it,
I write words
the way I have to when you hold me
captive with your eyes.

Spring Song

Snow falls silently upon frozen fescue—
begins when night shadows creep out
of the woods on their bellies
like hungry coyotes.
Large, the flakes sparkle in the red-orange
glow of the streetlight in the front yard.

I stand on the front porch, seeking truth
with a poet's blue-green eyes.
Wild flowers, in sleep, welcome the blanket
of white on towering Sewell bluff,
cicadas—years from birth—burrowed deep in the
land, do not know to fear the storm.

I know how to stalk the herd,
the flock, or the solitary wild word.
I come up quietly
the way a man approaches his lover
while she sleeps,
& bends over to kiss her.

Peering thru the dark,
I remember your radiance
when honeysuckle bloomed
along the roadside—
when your cheeks, flushed with sunlight
when the gnawing within my soul became a song.

You will wake today

without the usual alarm,
without your father waking first,
without your mother cooking breakfast,
& there will be no familiar sounds,
your fan that lulls you to sleep,
or traffic on the street
as your neighborhood wakes
& there will be no commute to work,
no lying in half darkness,
hating that daily drive.

At first,
you will not know where you are.
The bed, soft & warm, will not be
your bed.
Instead of the scent of candles,
wood smoke from a downstairs fireplace,
unmistakable cedar kindling
& popping sounds as flames grow,
will add to your confusion.

At first,
you may imagine the face
of a lover you desire
or recall how you made love,
or imagine the new lover
you pursue has seduced you.

Content, you might doze for a moment,
& escape from my poem
to wake today just as others do
around you in your house.

Waking, you will leave behind an empty space.
The distinctive tones of your voice,
like string instruments in a quartet,
you will take with you.

As for me,
I will write you back as sunlight
outside my A-frame wall of glass,
& the sound of leaves fanned in the wind,
& a finch singing notes of love
or I will write the two of us in the field
beneath the cliff
where the creek snakes thru it
& dew hangs on green fescue
like clouds to blue sky.

I woke this morning

remembering a literature teacher.
She was hell bent on teaching poetry,
introducing poets we had never heard
of in our Appalachian foothills.

There were stories told about her,
about how her trips to the cloakroom
meant sips of whiskey
quickly from a flask.

Thanatopis, Bryant's words were her favorite.
Memorizing them was our task,
especially the first eight lines
& the nine last.

After one trip to the back,
she came out reciting,
laying the words upon us:
So live

That when thy summons comes to join...
She hesitated, then took a different tack:
The cool wind
that stirs the stream in play, shall come to thee,

like one that loves
& then she stopped,
began to weep, recovered quoting:
Do not weep, maiden, for war is kind.

She popped her girdle,
But our love is stronger by far than the love
of those who were older than we
& we sat silent rather than risk her wrath.

& with a whine she muttered,
"Love yet stirs these old groins.
As for me, from me," she said:
Many red devils ran from my heart

And out upon the page.
And I recognized Poe:
While I weep—while I weep
and Crane:

They were so tiny
& tho she was tipsy
she finished with Whitman:
but every jot

of the greatness of man
is unfolded out of woman.

I knew a poet

who called
his muse
that gray eyed
skinny bitch
who never makes love

I knew a muse once
I called her simply
the word
& soft her skin was
upon the page

For a woman

I imagine you to be a red flower in the meadow,
one my eyes focus on
& take inside as the sun goes
along its way to other fields
where you will be in bloom,
towering above fescue.

In the passion play of Art & soft skin,
I imagine how you move in the wind, then
stand naked in the rain like a child,
laughing & dancing.

I imagine that you will survive
autumn in the meadow—
imagine my neighbor will not mow you,
but circle the place where you stand,
for he, too, will be taken in by you.

You are flower enough,
red brilliance enough,
to cause that little shift
I sense when memory mirrors you.

In winter as cold light
glimmers across Old Seventy Creek,
I will stand;
my face pressed against
an A-frame wall of glass;
my hand full of dried seeds.

To kill a word kills poetry

the Spanish conquistadors knew.
Their leader understood that
& knowing more burned his ship
upon arrival from Cuba
so his men could not mutiny—turn back
without gold, silver & other prizes
fit for royalty.

The Indians, fascinated by the large animals
upon which a man could ride,
& fearful of the white men's dogs of war,
told stories of a wealthy empire farther on
& up or so some conquistadors wrote in journals—
wrote how it amused them that the Aztecs
they found thought them messengers
from the gods—thought their leader, Cortes,
an armor-clad god to be honored
with gifts.

& the presents they gave him
were gold, the disease of the heart
that he sought.
Only when they had learned
as much of truth as they could stand,
did they rebel,
stop working their mines
to drive out the conquerors.

But it could not be done.
Cortes used cannons & guns
against the great Montezuma's warriors,
armed with bows & arrows tipped with stone
& shields made of hide.
But the greatest weapon Cortes used

was a native woman, Malinche,
who translated languages
& hated the Aztecs
& gathered her tribesmen,
non-believers in Huitzilopochtli,
the god of war, the sun,
the god hungry for hearts of virgins
& she hated more the warriors who placed them
still beating in the hands of priests,
human blood dripping at their feet,
food to lessen the insatiable hunger
that comes from chasing night
from the sky.

Malinche believed the sun would not die
if she could do away with human sacrifices.
She did not know to fear the invisible warriors
Cortes & his men brought: measles,
smallpox, mumps, typhus,
STDs with no glyphs to etch them in stones
or native names to talk about them.
The plague of death the white invaders brought,
she feared less than Huitzilopochtli.
& tho their diseases were not
the ring around the roses
all fall down dead variety
brought into Europe by fleas,
living on the horses of Mongol invaders,
her people & her enemies died by scores.
To kill the word,
Spaniards burned the libraries of Tenochtitlan,
left only untranslatable glyps in stone walls
to tell of the mighty empire,
to tell of the arts of war,
to keep the myths & legends mute.

Malinche,
I shall not curse you as others have
nor write your story in glyphs.
I shall not sing the songs your young men
sang to you, their words overflowing
between your breasts
then dripping onto the ground
to vanish.
In your bone jungle, birds sing
into a jungle canopy
& the arrowheads beneath the soil
sing of your betrayal.

For Heather

When I ask you
what do you want to know,

you say
*I want to know
everything there is to know
about you.*

I talk.
You listen.
You talk.
I listen.

There are things I cannot say
I tell you; yet,
I say more than I should
about pictures with names on the back.

And when I mention Reagan, you ask
did you like him?
I say *I did. He had a vision,
a plan to end Communism in Russia.*
You says *I did not like him*
I tell you about the Nicaraguan contras
about Lech Walesa and Pope John
then our political discussions cease.

I tell you
I can not explain how or
why I love women; say
*I only understand that each woman I meet
has a story that begs to be written.*
I see yours in your eyes.

I stand outside

Having no fear of dark places,
I stand outside.
Tho I have been gone two hours
beyond my normal work day,
I smell the smoke from the ash log
I placed on the grate
before I drove 127 north in daylight.

I listen to hurried feet, quick paces,
moving opposite thru the leaves. *Do not hide!*
Do not fear me! I call. *January buds—no flowers*
I tell myself—*will sway*
yellow come April. August fog
rising from Old Seventy Creek said snow
on this January date,
but what knows August of January? I ask. I write

flames that flicker upon the wind.
I write the touch of fingers along bare skin.
I write the singing of frogs along Old Seventy.
I write words across the black sky,
trying to piece together a poem,
trying to paint an image of a woman,
no child of forests, of open air;
but of intimacy, of indoor graces.

I close my eyes to light up the dark, bend
over you; uplift your small breasts when
I do as tho I am where my heart used to be;
as tho I am glancing over your shoulder; as tho I
seek your parted mouth to postpone
immortality & you, more than a kept woman,
welcome my most caressing look. You stare
into the stream of my eyes, one fish with two faces.

Or so the story goes

that men fear women,
unique ones, in particular,
fear them for they are strong,
fear the independent ones most,
the ones who know how not to sustain
male sexual identities
who know masculinity is no more important
to human erotic possibility
than poetry is to steep, Jack's Knob
or cold, flowing Old Seventy Creek.

& so the story ends
the way it began.

The last Sunday in February

As always,
when the wild geese fly north,
I count winter as having lost its grip
on the land.

As always,
I hear them before I see them. I look south
& east & find them, high in the clouds,
for they understand

they are targets, always
along the length of their flights chasing winter,
along their returning course, those heralds of spring.
Once, when I was a boy, thin but not tall,

our neighbor, a widower, grieving,
pointed his .22 toward the flock, firing:
rat, tat, tat-tat-tat-tat,
& a goose dropped near our house.

My brother & I ran to retrieve it.
Mother baked it.
Our neighbor joined us for dinner.
He ate & ate,

talking about his dead wife.
It was the first goose I ever ate.
I can't remember the taste of it.
I will always hear his voice tho

& always wonder
if the flock, floating that night
on Dale Hollow Lake, honked with grief
before they dived for shad minnows.

Early morning

I open my eyes.
A full moon shines thru
the skylight.
It occurs to me
how like a blank page
you are.
I want to write words
that touch all your secret
places & when you feel them,
I want my words
to sing a song you would write
for your ears alone.
I am reminded of Novalis
of Sophie who died young
& left her memory on his soul.
So alive she remained that he wrote hymns to her
about the night, the darkness
he knew as death.
Our yearnings make us brothers,
he & I.

I wrote a poem for you

on the chance you should visit
while I search the hills
or Old Seventy creek for words
where poets seldom walk.

I wonder what you will think of it,
door to my heart, both sills
unbolted so my words
are ever free to walk

away. If you find & read it
while I am gone, may chills
run thru you like deer herds
in the night & my yearning stalk

you like a lean coyote. Take it
& place it beneath your pillows,
for it is full of wild words.
that move silent as a hawk

& when they touch you
where you long
to be caressed,
you may send them back to me.

One day

when I got down & out,
blues heavy as red clay
on my shoes,
when spring threatened to
lose winter, you
point out the obvious: *I am quiet,
my poetry silenced.*

You pulled me up again.
I felt a surge of life
run thru me like Old Seventy creek.
I wrote a poem, a shouting mix of words
for pink almost exposed,
for fire,
the flames lovers relish,
the ones that burn inward,
outward, but never consume.

Man asked me:

*Do you think
you are a better poet
now?*

I think, I answer
*I have a voice these days
when I read my own words.
I never had that in the beginning.
My life has not been a drought
or something more destructive,
say a tornado,
or Wolf Creek Dam breaking,
taking out Burkesville,
flooding Nashville.
The truth is:
I see poetry these days
in a woman's eyes,
in daffodils along the road,
in my hidden past…*

& he interrupted me, asking:
*your hidden past, anything
you would change?*

I say:
*I would touch the woman
swim naked in Lake Cumberland at night
& I would never ruin a cause
nor betray what becomes of words
for anything.*

Daffodils

Daylight, sun rising on yellow trumpets, I
am reminded of a picture you sent me, one with you
framed by the camera's lens, naked, seductive & as
full of life as the frogs croaking poetry for spring
on the creek bank below me, water clear, flowing,
disappearing in a sinkhole beyond the trees.
I close my eyes & see you on your bed tan &
lithe, knees folded like a bud about to burst.
Suddenly, the wind has a chill to it.

I have a weakness

I have a weakness
for poetry—kind that hides
in shadows beneath Sewell Bluff—
naked in plain sight,
fragile,
colorless,
the way an Indian Pipe is.

I have a weakness
for women, Venus like in tides,
the ones who strut their stuff,
own the night,
argil,
unfired ones I guess.
It is

no difficult task
to surrender
to either weakness.
Lust is the purest vice
a man pursues
& love, the easiest
to lose.

I sit here

I sit here
alone;
my computer screen a white page;
my mind hungry for words;
& spring is but two days old.

Because I have been told
not to tell you, dear reader, words
of truth a woman less than half my age
revealed to me, I will tell you—the moon
in the west last night & the near

stars & the mist along Old Seventy Creek
& the yellow daffodils, too many to count
where once a log cabin stood,
a Tennessee rifle above the fireplace,
walnut mantle carved by an artisan—

all those things surely do not seek
to be hidden from men nor give account
to God in his good
glory. In the absence of such grace,
I learned to face my own fears. I understand

next to nothing of yours.

On Old Seventy Creek

On Old Seventy Creek, in water above my knees
& at a point where two streams rush—
where the gravel bar creates ripples
crossing the exposed roots of a sycamore—
I would paint a sprite, bathing shameless

& paint sunlight falling thru an opening in the trees;
paint hair that glistens—skin winter pale—& brush
foam on the water & her hands to hide her nipples;
paint a tilt to her head, & nothing more
& nothing less.

Whitney,

politics was to my father a measure,
a sky filled with illumination,
a big fish he might not land,
a new song to learn,
a walk thru familiar places.

Poetry was to me a pleasure,
a sudden realization,
a look at things I did not understand,
a new way to see, an unexpected turn,
a heart that races.

Where he had confidence,
I had desire.
Where he had victories,
I had a fire.
My poetry was a burning
he endured.

All the women I have never loved

All the women I have never loved,
I love on this night in March,
last night it is with fog rising
in the low field along the creek.

All the women I have never made love to,
I make love to in these lines, slow touching
each the way drops of occasional rain
ahead of a shower caress an upturned face.

Woman asked me:

*If you could have
any super power,
which would you choose?*

I thought for a moment & said:
I would choose to be invisible.

That's what I would choose
she said. *I wouldn't want
to be able to read minds.*

*Imagine what a torture
that would be*
I said.

& then I told myself
you would want to possess
the ability to read minds.

I would be invisible.
You would read my mind,
the poetry inside it

& you would stumble upon
the source of my desire
for words.

Within my innermost thoughts,
my feelings, the paint on the brush
is you .

The Visit

You showed me
the geese,
the wild Canadian ones
in the parking lot
where you work.

There is no water—
only black asphalt
stretched out like a sea.
The goose sits on her eggs
by the low shrubbery

far from the building.
The gander chases you
into & out of the building
each day
& pecks your car

as tho it were a cat.

Tho there is traffic

I observe you as I drive.
You toy with the power
your body holds over me.
Reclining the seat,
you lean back,
arms raised
the way they were
in another poem
in another book
You lower your left hand.
I am afraid you will hear
my pulse beating in my ears.
I do not speak,
for my voice would betray me.
I watch you.
Without looking back,
you know you have rekindled
my desire to write
what I know of poetry
upon your skin.

I plant seeds

The soil is wet
from yesterday's rain.
Tiny & black
the seeds are.

There will be flowers.
Come summer,
I will pick many bouquets
for you

& write poetry.

Do you think I am

you asked me
& before you said what it was
I was supposed to think you were, you said:

*People have always
told me I am,
my aunt says she always knew*

*& you—what do
you suppose I am?*

*I look at you
& see a woman
not a what* I say.

Risking the moment,
I add: *I feel masculine
in your presence.*

You sit silent.
*Do I take you home
or do I womannap you?* I ask.

Take me back you say.
*I have to work tomorrow
& earn money.*

Beautiful everywhere

You are a morning in spring
after storms rule the night.

You hold yellow sunlight
in your hands. Everything,

your lips, the tulips, the love song
finches in the tall oak sing,

not one note wrong,
Everything,

everywhere
beautiful
& you.

Even in the sky

you are, outlined by stars.
I see the faint one first
& I place it beneath you naval
few will think to look there
to find it.

& moving upward left
my gaze finds an equal star.
I place it beneath your right breast.

& moving right I see a brighter star,
perhaps a cluster of many stars
light years distant, burning out.
I place them just beyond your breast
on your ribcage.

& up, up, I place four stars,
illuminating your right breast,
three forming a perfect letter L,
with the fourth more in line
with the star I place near your lip.

Against the black that reaches beyond
the realm of rolling hillside,
the line of stars is poetry.
Even in the sky of night,
you are.

Freeze in April

After unseasonable heat
has warmed the land
& red buds have painted the hills
in their particular lavender
& dogwoods have painted their whites
& when iris with their swell of buds
like an aroused woman
threaten to bloom,
the freeze arrived.

Poplars,
yesterday festive in new growth green,
greet sunlight with blackened leaves,
as do all the trees,
as do all the tender iris,
heads bowed.

I stand in the yard.
Snow falls first one flake
then another,
then large flakes,
driven by the northwest wind,
claim the sky.

A red fox emerges from beneath
the old house
near the highway.
It is not the first time I have seen it,
but it is the only time it has not dashed away,
such is its confusion. I walk toward the A-frame

& somewhere in the endless corridors of my mind,
I hear your voice, singing.

I am in the woods
when you call.
I do not hear the cell phone,
for I placed it on a boulder
beneath the cliff
in vibrate mode.

Yesterday's freeze
yet blackens leaves
the length & width
of the steep hillside.
Old Seventy Creek flows

clear & cold
in the valley below.
I hear the beep of the phone
& I know I have missed a call
& I think it is you

& it is you.
I dial.
You are on the phone.
I leave a message.
You call me back

You ask:
what are you doing?
I'm looking for you I say.
& you say: *I am here* then you
tell me about your trip & your companion.

I ask: *Did you bring me a poem?*
There is silence.
A poem? You ask.
You always give me poetry I say
& then you understand.

I ask you:

*Does the way I write
offend you?*

& without hesitation
you say:

It does not offend me.

I sit beneath the cliff,
later,

looking down at Old Seventy Creek,
flowing as it has since my first

memory of it,
then looking up into the sky,

ever changing.

I would have stopped writing
your poetry, I tell myself,

if you had thought
me foolish.

You are a noiseless
magnetism.

I am pulled toward you like the cold
water below is tugged toward & over the falls.

Without shame,
I am proud

to be a poet again,
proud my real self

can come forth from me
& celebrate

words.

My visions of you,
invisible one,

are real as the wind
that brushes my cheek.

The voice I listen for,
far from me,

is as near to me
as the finch above me,

its yellow underbelly
bobbing on the limb

as it chants
one pure note

after another.

Far from lonely

            here in snow, alone
      eyelash distant
      from you.
      I am fire.

            See
                  me
                          burn!
            See
                  my
                          smoke

                  rise up

                  & disappear.

Muse

I hide you inside me,
words visible to inquisitive eyes,
& on lines that sing
silent betrayals
as they undress you & your skin
rises up with gooseflesh like watercress
on the hillside pond
an old man dug before my birth.

Come touch
my lips
my fingers
my fantasies.

Let me be a water strider.
moving quickly
moving quietly
moving surely
across the surface
of your deep, clear pool.

Greek Town, Chicago

Outside *The Greek Islands*
restaurant, the wind is brisk & cold.
I look up.
I see no stars.
I hear my inner voice asking:

why aren't you here?
I realize that I do not know
whether you like Greek food
& the ouzo hits me
hard.

I realize again that poetry
has your voice.
It dwells in me the way
the flow of Old Seventy Creek
dwells in me.
I can cup its water in my hands

but I can not keep its flow.
& so it is with you.
I can put your words
on a line
& down the page,

but your voice
moves on
& out always
a song, riding
red morning sunrise.

After rain

I listen to a finch,
outside the window of my office,
sending naked notes of a song
into the world.

I hear a wren protest
as tho a cat, crouched,
moves about the yard
too close to its nest.

I hear a martin,
a voice from my past,
join the chorus
& a cardinal.

I get up.
I walk to the window;
part the horizontal blind
& find

a mockingbird in the oak,
silent,
its repertoire
exhausted.

Iris

Protected by the overhang
on the east side of the A-frame,
an iris, salmon mixed with yellow,
blooms while trees shed leaves,
brown oak & black hickory,
frozen in late April.

If a muse hears her poet,
she knows already that I think
to cut it long-stemmed,
place it in a poem,
a fragile vase of words
filled half-way up with water

& call it beautiful.

Too tired to write,

I close my eyes & I see you as you were
in pictures that you shared.
I hear your voice in song,
amazingly strong.

I touch you as I have never touched you,
the way my fingers caress a keyboard,
writing words without thinking,
feeling each syllable as tho it were

a cheek,
a nipple,
the bend of your leg,
the rushing water of Old Seventy Creek.

If I could touch you

I would choose spring
to do it.
I would choose to be God
& reach down from the naked
branches of a wild peach tree
in bloom.

I would choose spring
when happiness returns
& be God
& I would touch you
with my finger of warm breezes
& fill the hole in your heart

with orchids.

The Bad Boy

Book Two

The bad boy

I have never told you the story
about the first woman I met
when I came to Kentucky
when I was a bad boy,
have I?

No
I say.

She was married,
separated,
waiting for her divorce.
After we finished she said
I have one word for you: virile.

You were a bad boy
I say
a good bad boy.

That night you say
I dreamed I looked up
the clouds parted
& there was Jesus
& he said

I can't let you come in here
for that thing
you have done.

We went out other times
you said
I could never touch her
after that.

Writers

When **the bad boy** says to
the big man: *yesterday (*calling her by name*)*
wore red panties,
the big man asks:
you mean the one born in (saying the country)
& raised in (saying another country)?

You know the one I mean **the bad boy says.**
The one who plays (mentioning a sport)? **the big
man asks.**
The good-looking one **the bad boy** answers.
The skirt she wore was so short
& her panties were red.

You mean (mentioning both her names)? I ask.
I sat across from her yesterday during lunch.
The conversation ended at once.
I do not tell them, **the bad boy** & **the big man**,
that when she stood up I thought:
There has to be a poem in this.
I never expected the two of them would write it.

The ones I never

I did not tell
the bad boy
& the big man
how their conversation
brought back memories
that flashed thru me
in a moment.

I did not tell them how in high school, the blond,
across from me in science class,
turned my way during lectures,
& I can hear the teacher's monotone voice
to this day. Boring as watching grass grow,
it was, but the blonde
when she put her feet in the book compartment
of the desk, would wait to catch my eye,
smile, spread her legs,
& one day wore no panties!

I did not take time to tell them
I was not fond enough
of the girl in the bleachers
at our baseball games to go to her
when she would send word to me
that she liked me
& would I come
sit with her.

& in that moment I could have told them
about the young lady at Grider Hill dock,
aboard her father's houseboat,
who dropped her top & asked me
how does it feel to be shot
by a pair of thirty-eights?

I never got to answer,
for her parents walked up
& I dived into Lake Cumberland
to hide in its warm wetness.

& in that moment I could have told them
about my friend, older than me by more than six
years, who talked about his girls,
who would get naked
at the drop of a hat
& always said *I would show you how,
but you don't wear one.*

& in that moment I could have told them
about the wild, West Virginia coal miner's daughter
I never did who had a lesbian lover
& a boyfriend she later married
nor did I mention her sister who was straight
& for sure I never mentioned the ugly girls
my college buddy, Terry dated because he said:
*They are easy
& always thankful afterwards.*

If the moment had not been so short,
I might have told them about the young lady on the
cruise ship between Greek islands
who came up to the deck
& sat on the bench beside me—having gotten
seasick in the lower dining quarters
from the heavy rock & roll
of the ship in the 93 knots tempest,
who came up sicker with the fear of dying.
You are one crazy poet she said
to sit up here like this.
I might have told them how she leaned
her head on my shoulder or how

water leaped the railing, drenching us
like we were part of the cast
in a black & white Errol Flynn movie.
Perhaps we would have laughed together had I told
them when we docked at Mikinos she asked:
Do you know what would look good on you?
& I said: *No.*
Me with nothing on she said
& rode up the steep hill
on a donkey & I never saw her again.

I could have told them there was the lady in the
Atlanta airport during a nine-hour layover
when a tornado hit the city who asked:
Will you watch over me so I can rest?
Said: *I am exhausted, afraid of airports,*
& I don't want to be raped.
I could have told them how I agreed
& how she smiled, then slept on the floor,
one arm around my leg.
I could have told them how I woke her in time
for her to catch her flight & how she took time to
write on a piece of paper, the words:
My phone number
in case you ever get to Knoxville is...

Perhaps they knew already
the story about the woman in Brazil,
the one who came up to me in the disco,
speaking Portuguese & sat down unaware that I had
a government issued **Colt**
between my legs
& my right foot on a duffel bag stuffed
with **Banco Brasilia** banknotes & perhaps
they knew that she reached beneath the table
& grabbed my pistol then ran away, screaming.

The students I never told them about
I might have mentioned:
one who knew too much of police matters
who asked for my help which I gave
to save her life
& the one who asked
when are we going out on a date? I could have told
them that we never…

I could have told them about the night
in the red light district in Amsterdam
when I saw a black-haired beauty
in a window, naked, & how her sad eyes
told a story I could not change
by walking inside nor walking away
which I did. For sure, I could have told them
of the nude German girl in the Chinese Gardens
in Munich who shouted up to me in German:
*I am teasing the old man on the bridge
because I like his beard* and asked
maybe do you like this body, too?
For in that moment, I remember shouting back in
German: *Sicher*.
& remember how dumbfounded she looked...

& in that moment at the table, I could have told
them other realities
but the fact
that no one who retells the events
in my life ever wants to let truth destroy
a great story held me back.

The bad boy said one day

during lunch
I am not like most men.
I like breasts.
Have I ever told you
he asked
how God stole my girlfriend?

No
I said
tell me.

We were in Ireland
& I noticed her
but I was too much in love

he said
with a girl.
We planned to meet in London
when summer was over.
How the girl in Ireland could sing.
She could sing opera
& she had big breasts
& showed them off,
but kept them covered,
for she was a good,
Christian girl.
& she was small—
her waist
he said,
finishing nonverbally
with his hands as tho
encircling her torso.

*We would do dishes
together in the kitchen
& go down to the beach later
& jump over sand dunes.
Doing that on our last nigh together,,
she came up behind me—
put her arms around me—
kissed me on the cheek*
he said,
placing his right finger
on that left cheek memory
then pointing at his ear
she whispered into it:
**I love you,
but I love God more.**

Request

Send me words
& I will hold them
in my hand until they burn
my skin
like red, glowing coals
then

I will toss them
into the air
& in falling
they will cool
& land on the white page
in disarray.

Eyes closed,
I will stir them
with my finger
until they sing
like the wind
thru pine needles.

A Small Poem

All the perversions of the soul
I wrote in a small poem.
How to do harm to women
& be harmed by women;
how to love;
how to be out of love.

Attracted always to their tragedies,
I wrote the real or imagined,
their bitterness over giving up
their bodies to men,
their one-time first time,
their wanting to call back dire regrets.

Always listening to those regrets,
I wrote their songs without words or rhyme,
their unwritten histories—women
only quail, rising up,
unaware they will be gunned
down above the weeds. Tragedies

& other lovely things, love,
men who know the flights of birds, love,
the end of beauty & attachments to men, I wrote.
It was a small poem,
only large enough to hold
all the perversions of the soul.

In his journal

on September 1,
the monk, Thomas Merton,
wrote words,
confessing his desire
to be a saint.

He had taken a vow of poverty,
of silence,
of working with his hands.
He was, however, a poet.
His words buzzed like bees.

All that is possible

I would confess
that I noticed you
& my first thought
had to do with
the way your long hair,
[curls,
fashionably,
palpably wet]
reminded me of
Titian's—not Botticelli's—ideal
of beauty,
his Venus Rising from the sea.

& I would confess
that I noticed you
& told myself I ought
not allow your face, with
one glance, to snare
me, but a feeling unfurls,
suddenly,
& I get,
noticeably unbalanced, of
course I feel,
uncomfortably sure you see
thru me.

I realize, in a poet's way,
that you are woman enough
to know that I truly love
the company I keep.
In the meeting of our eyes,
yours are as transparent as
the narrow creek in front of
my grandparents' house,
only the water striders
are absent. In them,
I see all that is possible for you;
another poem rising from me.

I know the secret corner

where you dwell,
where you wait,
impatiently,
for music
& song.
I know how you long to moan
be a whisper lost to ear,
be one of two bodies,
breathing rapidly,
be a light snow
falling in the dark.

Watching Old Seventy Creek

flow down its course,
then moving with its running,
but at a slow pace,

I turn to face a waterfall,
no taller than I am tall,
then I sit on moss-covered stone

in that stream,
the water going past me
like a dream to either side.

Sun on my face,
silence, the sound of rushing,
like new lovers in the air

around about me.
My feelings swim thru rapids,
like a snail darter.

Hiking

I walk,
sunlight my companion
along Old Seventy Creek.

Wildflowers
hold onto the cliffs,
their whites,

their pinks,
their blues
newly bloomed.

Water striders
walk on water
in still pools.

They are
the only true poets
I encounter.

I remember the too hot day in April

when tender buds in their swelling
rush to leave winter,
in their eager want for new growth green,
were innocents,
intent on making love. I understand

well that intention, but I remember telling
myself how cold the hand
of icy fingers, the mean
streak of winter,
are; but those innocents,

those showy limbs
turned black during the night.
It will be a year of no peaches,
their juice dripping
from the corners of our mouths;

no sweet taste lingering
on our lips.

Nickname

I call her dynamite.
Her beauty is quiet,
iris blooms unfurling
in May
&
explosive,
fiery sunset
end to day.

I will write you

wet like Old Seventy Creek
from its beginning
to its end.

I will write you
into my poem
& a shiver will run
down my spine,

for I will write you
lovely as the far mountains
succulent as honeysuckle nectar
& in your eyes

I will write the reflection
of a quarter moon
& in your ears the summer night song
of a whippoorwill.

Once on Lick Branch

I found plums
& sweet they were,
for in a past life
they were tame.
Perhaps a raccoon
carried one to the bluffs
& ate its fruit
then dropped a seed.
Perhaps a tree grew,
leaning
over Lick Branch,
its cold water
washing its fallen fruit
clean
& fate would find me
eating them there
in darkness.

I would have saved some
that night from the water
& brought them to you
& squeezed one
so its juice
ran as far as my desire
along your body,
but they were so ripe,
so cold,
& so very few.
I ate them slowly
in spite of myself.
I did not know at the time
that plums were your favorite
of all God's forbidden fruits.

Poetry is a Mountain

steep toward the summit
like Jack's Knob. Sunlight
& words flow
thru valleys rapid as a stream
after spring rain
& disappear.

I climb the mountain
& sit on the summit
of it, alone, write
words wild enough to go
silent thru fog or dream
past joy, pain,
& reappear

wherever it is
you are.

Let me give you

all that I am
in words
for words know how
fog settles on Old Seventy creek
in the hour before the sun
burns thru

& words know dew on winter wheat,
knee high,
know honeysuckle wrapped around wire
know the song a Martin sings in spring,
the feel of soil turned upright by the plow
& words are seeds

& words are mountains,
ridges, rolling slopes,
or land so level the eye can not see
to its horizon
& words are water, flowing,
a blue hole where Red Horse spawn,
so cold a reader's teeth chatter
at first plunge into it
& lips discolor

& words are flat rocks warmed in midday sun
& sky above, endless,
but more than words
I cannot control.

My words

When I write,
my words flow from me,
warm enough to melt snow
from your heart—full of life,
moving out, carrying hopes,
dreams, sullies
of meanings like Muse creek,
muddy after rain
& lovers' lips tight pressed.

My words, undressed,
are eagles above the plain,
soaring, full of life—
are tears upon a cheek,
are gullies
on red clay slopes,
crooking down & around. See
how they go,
slithering snakelike thru the night!

If there is reason
or there is rhyme
to my poetry,
let there also be passion,
hot to the touch
& full of lust.

I re(a)d a poem

I re(a)d a poem
(one by
the bad boy
of American poetry
who made you smile)
smile as tho
his words were lips
kissing your lips
as tho they were
his lips kissing
your body
as tho they were
his fingers
ever so softly
moving in circles
like a moth
around
hot light

….his lips
his fingers
your body
your smile
& me watching
the two of you
you reading
his words writing
that smile
on your lips
in broad daylight

When I pop the cork,

scent floods
my soul with remembering—
the art of it
& there is an art to it
or there is nothing.

I close my eyes,
attempting to write the aroma,
the passion upon my tongue
as I caress its fruity taste
with pursing lips.

I lower my glass.
The scent returns;
I burn, sucking in air
as tho it were a woman's breath
in a dark room.

I sip again
& hold the sensitive swell
afraid to move,
recalling an intimate moment
as tho it were a dream.

A dog barks,
far off, muffled by the trees
& the glass in my hand
is only a glass
& the wine is suddenly ordinary.

Speed Museum, Louisville

I look at the painting again
then Einstein's words hit me,
making more sense to me
than his scientific equations
& his theory ever did.

He saw past the skin of us,
watching lines of museum
passersby
& saw a kind of prison,
restricting personal desires
& affections.
He could pick out
the imprisoned ones
of us without fail.

I search eyes
for the same reason.
In yours, a smoldering
woman resides.

Writing your poetry

is like balancing a rocker
so it leans backward
an improbable distance
without tipping over—

is like walking a log
across Old Seventy creek—
taking slow steps—
pausing to breathe.

A sonnet is the form

that thinking gravitates toward:
da dum da dum da dum da dum da dum.

But feelings are a
la di da

across then down a line they go
& begin to dance.

Passion simply sings shape notes:
do re mi fa sol la ti do

or backward go
do sol me do.

I remember rain on a tin roof
in my youth

when I lay in the hay loft
longing to be a drummer,

with long hair
& no worries

mate.

A red car

passed me
when I was driving
in a daze,
trying to write poetry
in my head.

An arm waved
from the passenger's side,
kept waving,
waving,
until I waved, too

& when the driver
made a quick
left turn,
I recognized her,
for she was a muse.

Braking, I turned left,
thinking less
about the words unwritten
as the red car
backed up toward me.

Walking
toward that car,
I felt my heart pound
& I realized I had been writing
the wrong poem.

In the car,
three young women,
alive, chattering,
voices vibrant speaking as one
were all I heard,

& looking down,
the driver's tan legs
were all I saw
until she stuck her head out,
talking incessantly.

When she sat,
all I could see again was skin,
smooth as a polished line in a poem,
& I knew without a doubt
that the words I had wanted to write, those seeking

a universe had found their mooring.

A pony

broke free
from its hobble
one night
when the horse *coper*
lay intoxicated
in his tent.

Running in moonlight
across the desert,
the pony
smelled the river
in the distance
& jasmine, flowering white.

When the owner woke,
he gave chase on a camel
like a jealous lover,
tracking the pony
across the sand,
determined to bring his property home.

By the river,
a woman sat,
committing poetry
to memory.
She, as well,
was out of her corral.

She saw the pony pause
to drink deeply
from the river
& heard the camel
approaching,
loud in its protest.

The pony took to the river,
swimming with the flow,
& the moon,
losing its glow to black
before dawn,
covered the escape.

The woman hid
in the meadow
like a roe
among lilacs
while the horse trader
cursed his fate.

While
sunlight
committed another poem
of life to memory,
the woman bathed
in flowing water.

If I never

write a poem that excites
a reader the way you cause me
to tremble inside
at the mere thought
of
(I will not mention
more
except to say,

Old Seventy creek is
no more beautiful in its way
than your eyes when you do not divert them
tho its water captures open sky.
It is no less beautiful than your body
I can never touch).

I will touch it with words,
hesitating ones,
words tightly pressing
against your softness,
words that are fingers
& lips exploring the vastness,
the unmapped universe
of the page
upon which you lie.

The Moon is Amazing

again tonight,
but no more so
than the memory
of you

that travels an orbit
inside me
& bends my poetry
toward the windows

upon which I write.
Cool air, warm room
fogs them, makes them ready
for my words.

You toss me
like ocean waves
& pull me back
into myself

as you spin
farther,
faster
away.

I sit opposite you,

listening to your voice
as you talk about your friend,
the one moving to Ohio

asking me if you should go
Friday night or spend
the night Saturday. *My choice*

I answer *depends on how you will feel*
after the move when you are here alone.
You say *Sad.*

I tell you *Too bad.*
Go beyond your comfort zone.
If life, if love, if lust is real,

stay both nights & the day between
I say & the keen, clear look of open skies
leaps back into your eyes.

The Picture You Sent

Black enamel headboard
against a white wall
& in the upper left
corner
on the bedpost
one pair of
blue
see thru
thong
panties

Iris in bloom

Having no regard
for the fact
that the red
clay bank
along the highway
is in no manner
or stretch
of the imagination
a garden,
you send stems upward
with not one,
not two,
but three bearded
flowers,
royal purple
& velvet white.

Soft Places

I asked you
if you had soft places
for me to cry on,

you hesitated,
wanted to know
what I meant.

I told you—
you understood,
for shoulders are hard.

Words I write for you
do not come easy like the ones
I craft on lines for Old Seventy creek.

I know the stream;
its ways; its mysteries—
know how fog rises from it

then dissipates.
I have swum in the deep pools
where the stream from the MacFarland farm

joins its flow.
I have stood in the openings
& closings of its caves

& walked thru the sinks
beneath the highway,
my footprints preserved in mud.

I know its wild flowers;
its song birds;
& its rhythm.

Old Seventy writes poetry
in a voice that ripples downstream
beneath the hardwood trees

& off the page.

The poem's charge

Tell her she is unique. Tell her
she lives in my words. Tell her
that her face has no pain, as she
remembers it within those lines.

Tell her many words wait. Tell her
I must write them one by one. Tell her
the praying mantis eats them. She
will understand. Tell her the pines

are infected with beetles. Tell her
Old Seventy creek runs swift. Tell her
its cold water flows over stones she
will never see. Tell her the confines

of my mind contain—tell her—
hundreds & hundreds—tell her—
of ideas for poems. She
is curled around their images, their wines

are Riesling sweet.

Tired, stressed

I sit in front of the computer screen
& close my eyes, thinking to feel you
enough to write a poem.

I hear a voice—not my own—not
yours, but a woman's voice,
muffled, & all I hear in all she says

is:
I am Old Seventy creek.
My curves are a woman's...

I long to put a face with her voice.
I search memory & old desires.
My eyelids get so heavy I cannot open them.

A funnel cloud cuts a path
across the landscape in my eyes. Pines,
poplars & mighty oaks fall.

I see every poem I ever wrote
sucked up on their pages
to get tossed out one word after the next.

I see me crawling behind the black cloud
with a bucket, a dust pan
& a broom.

Elaine

I cannot write words
that will ease the pain
of your death.

I cannot write my tears
along a line
nor down a page.

Before November 9, 1965,
there was a void in the world
& you filled it the next day being born.

When our father died,
an emptiness grew inside me,
heavy as a brown-skinned creek rock.

When our mother died,
a second emptiness formed beside the first.
It too felt heavy; I carry it tho.

This third emptiness…
This third heaviness…
How it bows my back.

Gary's Dream

"When Gay called me,
I was dreaming of Elaine.
Pa and me and Uncle Maxie
were at church taking turns leading the singing.
It was one of those all-day affairs.
All at once, Elaine gets up and sings.
It was a song I did not know,
and I know many,
but she sang it,
never missing a word.
Then the phone rang—maybe 4:30
in the morning and Gay said she was dead.

About two weeks later,
I had a dream.
Elaine was below the dam at a pay phone.
Next thing I know, she's driving across the dam
and I can see her plain—hear her crying—see her
tears, then I see the wall and the smoke rising
when she hits it.
I always wake up at that moment.
I must have had that same dream 35 or 40 times.
It never changes.
I can close my eyes now
and see it,
but I can't understand…"

Aunt Mary Wood

I came to you
without flowers

& Gary, your son,
asleep in the recliner

by the window
wore your pain, too.

I did not wake him.
I listened to your breath

the struggle of it
& I remembered Gathie

straining like that
when she sent for me

& I remembered Mom
the night I sat by her

before her last morning.

I took a wet cloth
& wiped your forehead.

I pushed your hair
from your eyes.

You woke, smiling,
talking.

You called me by my father's name.
Gary woke at half past midnight.

so what if lust comes

first
& love never
happens tho
your thighs
your tan lines
blend into poetry
& your words come
tho you are thinking
they know not how
to spasm in their all

I thirst
my blood rushes ever
gushes & so
where your sighs
go (them entwines
my arm loosely)
as your numb-
ing
eyelids flutter (now
write your poem! you call)

Out.

Writing a novel

Robert Penn Warren said
he gave up writing novels when
he realized they
took too much time
away from writing poetry.

Like Anna Akhmatova, the
Russian poetess whose rhyme
holds me sway,
I wait at night for words then
scribble notes within my head.

It is as tho I have no voice
except the words in my fingers.
If they come out as prose,
it is as tho I keep the sin some
call passion locked inside.

The sounds refuse to hide
& always overcome
the novel of my moment. A word goes
out from my sentence & lingers
like lips against a nipple. I must rejoice.

Let me sin
that I might breathe again.

When I write poetry,

I capture the sound of longing;
a sound only God hears
before fingers touch skin,
before lips moisten neck,
before words line up
naked across the page
to dance with the deviltry
of an epiphany.

I know

that you see
where my eyes go
when they are
martins gliding
on air in April.

I know you understand
why I have traded myself
without hesitation for another
& tho you question
whether the one I traded with

is capable of such a miracle,
I cannot risk such questioning,
for truth has set me free.
I understand I no longer risk heaven
when I grow weak in your presence.

Wind

Wind,
old friend,
old enemy,
I hear you.

Your howl is bestial.
You roll clouds,
not yet black,
building patiently

until late afternoon.
When night falls,
you grow calm
for the time

it takes you
to rotate,
then drop
the funnel…

I asked the bad boy

if he had any stories for me,
the kind only he can tell.

I think he said
I'm going to keep

all my stories
for when I write

my book.

Except for the—
he got an Oh Hell

look on his face—I said
ones cut deep

into the pages of my book. Stories
you told me I might

use. He got that look

on his face again,
but he smiled.

Tending Fires

Book Three

Snowflakes fall, drift

I watch them.
I go outside & bring in
as much wood
as I can carry.

I sit down & drift
into my feelings.
I recall the day
a teacher encouraged me

to write poetry
& tho everyone around
about me saw no crystal muse,
I saw her.

How she could dance,
& how she could sing,
that muse, for me
& I believed

that no one could possess her.
& I remember how the fragrance
she wore was pure seduction,
I remember saying:

how like honeysuckle
to myself.
The smell lingers,
& the snowflakes fall, drift.

In reality & in dreams

The fire burns low;
the room cools.
I remember the day
she first aroused me.

She noticed me,
studying her,
looking for words,
for a poem.

She smiled. I wake.
I get up,
fetch more firewood,
& when I sit down,

I recall:
she did not smile for me.
I fall asleep.
I dream.

I dream about the women
my father hired by the hour,
& how they would work
for a quarter of a dollar.

Those women dug grass,
red careless weeds,
but mostly crabgrass
from fragile tobacco plants.

My father called them
his 25 cent hoers.
He loved them enough
to make such a joke.

Dreams fulfill but are not fulfillment

I wake.
My father & the women he loved,
the woman, my mother
who loved him—all are dead.

I faced reality
when that teacher
introduced me to poetry.
At night, I searched my feelings,

but the young man I was
lacked points of reference.
I can look back into time
& see an old woman,

raising her cane,
threatening me crossing her lawn,
saying: *don't you know better
than lollygag round hyar?*

She told me:
you'll come to no count
& I told her I had thoughts
of being a poet.

No good she said
*can come from that.
Don't let me ketch you
round hyar no more!*

I remember a smile

the way I remember
the first poet I heard read from his works.
I was so jealous of him
for having a muse to pinch his cheek

that I only heard his rhyme.
I wished for a muse, however,
& afterwards at the reception,
he shook my hand violently

& I remember thinking:
perhaps his muse will fall off his shoulders,
for I imagined she had that same knowing smile
of curiosity upon her face that you have

& I imagined her:
as you clinging tight to my words.

One day I will write a poem

about that smile,
about the fragrance,
but I realize a poet must write
from experience

& convince everyone else
he doesn't.
Having had no luck
preserving a smile in words,

yours will be a difficult poem
to embrace.

Snowflakes stop falling, melt

I will write a poem,
not about smiles,
not about honeysuckle,
but about a friend,

one who died in the war,
died a hero in a jungle
& I will write how a part of me
died, too.

I will put myself into my words
& they will waltz across the page.
I will cry when I read them
in front of my mirror.

Snowflakes stop falling, melt,
& the room grows cold again.

When I submitted my first poems,

the editor was polite,
writing back:
try again...
some lines are good.

I tried again.
Refreshing he wrote back
but I am overstocked
with words at the moment.

& when I sent another batch,
he wrote: *these should be*
chalked up to experience
& not even reworked.

He suggested that I should:
try to find my own voice.

My voice hid from me

until one day I wrote a poem,
one with rhyme about the war;
it was published,
then I wrote a poem

about my neighbor.
My voice no longer hid from me.
I no longer was a parody,
no longer wrote jagged lines

that broke in the wrong places.
I submitted the poem;
it was published.
It did not rhyme.

I let my best friend read it.
For some reason,
he saw his reflection
as tho my words were a mirror.

*So that's what you really
think of me?*
he asked
and stomped off.

The fire burns low, only coals glow

When I thought I was going to be drafted,
I remember I told my friends:
I'm a poet.
A few of them congratulated me.

I let those few read my works.
They shook their head in approval.
I'm a poet I said.
One of them said *Nobody wants to read that.*

They all laughed.
*Can't you recognize a poet
when you see one?*
I asked.

No the one of them answered
*but anyone can recognize
that poetry is just another whore.*
I woke again.

The fire burns low,
only a few coals glow.

It was the coldest day of the year

The wind had the teeth of an editor.
I rekindled the fire.
I sat down, my fingers red chilled.
I closed my eyes.

I could see my brother, Gary
& I could see me.
We were upstairs in the old house
in the hollow, living where my father

was born.
I heard his voice saying,
on the coldest day of winter,
snow would blow under the shingles.

I could see us, upstairs,
with snow drifting down,
settling white on our covers,
& the glass of water my brother

brought up with him,
frozen on the nightstand.

An editor said:

yes I'll take one;
publish it;
pay in copies,
& I never told anyone.

I read it for my muse.
I read it silently for my brother
& my sisters,
my father & my mother.

& then I finally read it
aloud, for myself.

Quentin Howard, editor of *Wind*, wrote:

Some of these are very, very good.
But hold off a while;
try me again
in September.

I held off, but kept writing.
It was as tho my muse
had moved in;
pushed my clothes to one side

of the closet.
Just when I told myself:
poets get tired of waiting
to be discovered,

Quentin wrote:
I used your poems.
Get me a manuscript
& I will publish a book.

I sent Quentin a manuscript

Yes
he wrote back.
In particular,
I like the poem

about death,
one of the oldest
universal feelings
he wrote.

Imagine a ping-pong player
he wrote.
One whose serve changes
direction like the wind.

Your poem is like that.
I never heard from him again.
Years later, I found out
a coal truck crashed into his car.

He and my manuscript
both died that day.

Interview

What are your qualifications?
the superintendent asked me.

Words I said
& a feeling for them.

I understand he said
you were set to be drafted.

It's a helluva war
he said.

I nodded.
He looked at me.

There have been two poets
he said *in this county.*

One was queer.
The other was sneered at...

One lies in the town cemetery;
the other had his works published.

Anything else you do? he asked.
Not as well, I said.

Your father is one of my best friends.
He gets votes regular as a sow gets pigs.

I nodded.
I'm sure I can find something for you to do,

he said.

While the fire roared,

I piled more wood on the flames.
Snow fell, drifting.
I sat in the swivel rocker,
drifting into sleep.

What is that? a girl's voice
came to me. I see her.
Just poetry, I said
when I finished reading.

Teach us, the girl said
to write.
I'll try, I said
& I did.

The girl wrote a poem.
It was personal,
confessional.
She read it to the class.

Next day,
an irate parent came to school.
*You might as well have a whore
sitting on your desk with her legs spread,*

she said *as let the kids hear
something like that.*

Acceptance

*She was wrong
to come here like that,* I hear
the girl's voice the one
whose mother raised hell

say.
Read to us again
she says
& let us read to each other

that we might learn.
I warned them:
*few are they who trust a man
or a woman who twists words*

*into poetry like corn leaves
during drought.
A poet is neither trusted
nor understood.*

But I read to them
& they wrote
& they read to each other
& thereafter,

no parent dropped by to criticize.

Writing lesson

You must keep reading poetry
to be able to write it, I taught.
You must be able to write words
that do not look like poetry;

words that may not sound like poetry.
You must say more
by saying less.
I told them.

I told them what Jim Wayne Miller
had said about writers:
Don't be satisfied with what you say,
until you are ready

to carve your words
in stone.
I watched them shatter
stone after stone,

but not one of them
took a chisel in hand
& carved a statue of a whore,
seated on a desk with legs spread.

Night

I get up;
close the glass doors
to capture
& keep the fire.

I make my bed
on the sofa.
It will be a long night,
colder than the day.

& I will be up
many times,
carrying firewood thru snow
& I will dream many dreams

& in one of my dreams,
the lilies on the roadside,
unafraid of the frozen earth
will become women who love men

& I will become the man
who loves their blooms
& writes them as poetry
across the page, then down.

If I up

[enter]
on
[ing]
 You
& find
out how?
 Good
your [dan]
[ce]
to music
is

[evil&
without =]

do Not
Wish
to Remove
[the drum&
roll
thund-
erous
two twirls
of drum&
sticks]
Me from

In&
Side
your soli[t
ary]
Con
[fine]
ment

Moonlight

thru the A-frame wall of glass,
framed, its brilliance
almost equal to a woman's,
but not equal
to those women
I seem to admire
or touch;
the few I have loved
whose eyes capture the moon
like Old Seventy Creek can.
How many times,
I have gazed into the depth
of that water,
having understood
none of the least of it
until this moment.

I want to dream

the dream I had two
nights in a row, tho
I know I cannot do
it.

I want to be
an azure sea,
rolling in
& out & in
again

to caress your skin.

Confession

Hollis Summers told me:
*I like the way your poetry
reflects women.
Your words help me
understand why
T. S. Eliot regarded
every poem as a temptation
& would not write one
for years
& why I rush to get mine
on the line.*

www.ingramcontent.com/pod-product-compliance
Lightning Source LLC
Chambersburg PA
CBHW031647040426
42453CB00006B/242